AF575187

Jo-

Happy Birthday!!

Thanks for everything-

your support, your humor, your

stories, and especially your

lunch-time chocolaty candy treats you

always share with everyone!!

Happy 50th! (from a science geek

to a math nerd)

your friend,

Sue

What Do Women REALLY Want? Chocolate!

Donna L. Barstow

Foreword by
Rose Levy Beranbaum
("The Cake Bible")

NANTIER · BEALL · MINOUSTCHINE
Publishing inc.
new york

ISBN 1-56163-383-6

Printed in China

3 2 1

Introduction

by Rose Levy Beranbaum

Best-selling author of *The Cake Bible*

The finest compliment I have ever received was from my friend Howard Helmer, who has been listed several times in the Guinness Book of World Records as the world's fastest omelet maker. But he doesn't just make them fast, he also makes them funny, because Helmer is a natural-born, world-class comedic performer. So when he told me that I was the most ridiculous person he knew, I was delighted! I pride myself on having a finely-tuned sense of the absurd and am always ready to hazard a play on words. Even a former cleaning lady once suggested a career as a standup comic (and NO, I hadn't asked her to wash the windows!). People have always found me funny so I've given a lot of thought, over the years, as to the different sorts and degrees of humor-exactly what makes something funny, especially to the point of uncontrollable laughter, perhaps best described as the orgasm of the soul. Laughter is terribly personal. What people laugh about defines them because it emanates from the deepest truest reality of a person's being. It's one thing you really can't fake (what sounds more pathetic than forced laughter?).

As far as I'm concerned, nothing, including tragedy, is exempt from the possibility of a joke, buried somewhere within it. In fact, the worse things get, the more likely I am to find them in some way humorous. Maybe it's my upbringing in the Jewish tradition of survival through laughter. I'll always remember reaching my 82 year old senile mother through a desperate leap of humor when my father asked me to assure her that she could no longer get pregnant. "Ma! I cried out, "Why didn't I think of it: you could have the baby for me." She immediately caught the laser double-edged dart of irony and laughed. Laughter, like chocolate, can be bitter-sweet. But is there a more delicious pleasure than a great long laugh? Well, maybe chocolate. So what could be a more irresistible honor than an invitation to write the foreword to this terrific book that dares to combine the two! But why not? Perhaps what chocolate and humor both have most profoundly in common is that they satisfy in a deep-down sort of way. And by doing so they heal us and make us whole time and time again.

A chocolate memory I hold dear is when I was on book tour in S.F. for the French chocolate book I translated and revised, "A Passion for Chocolate." The day after the big earthquake hit, I called my mother in NewYork to reassure her that her only two children (the other one, my brother, lives in the Bay Area), had survived. But she would hear none of it in her eagerness to impart the news she had just read in her dental journal that she was certain would help sell the book: "Chocolate helps prevent tooth decay!" The San Franciscans, however, had another message for me: "Next time, leave your passion at home!" they teased.

The art of the cartoon is a unique form of humor. At its best it is a sharply focused poetic merging of artistic vision and intellect. To my mind, it is the ultimate eloquence. It is seeing something so clearly one laughs with a burst of glad recognition. Great cartooning hits a nerve. It doesn't always make us laugh out loud, but when it works, it provokes us into seeing the world in a different way. It kaleidoscopes our vision. It is a pointed statement or satire of our values and our times. I recognized that I had reached a major saturation pinnacle in my career, when, to my total surprise, I found my name and signature "Lemon Poppyseed Pound Cake" from "The Cake Bible" in a "Flight Deck" cartoon by Peter Waldner!

What I enjoy most about Donna Barstow's cartoons, is that in just one whimsical drawing, and one well-chosen phrase, I get the full impact of a whole story complete with subtext and history that taps me directly into my own memories and associations. This delightful book is replete with chocolate and social commentary. I invite you to sit down, with a box or bar of your favorite chocolate, and bliss your way through a deliciously hilarious read. Why the chocolate? Because while making you smile and roar with laughter, these cartoons will also make you very, very hungry for the stuff. And as one of my favorite cartoons in the book reads: "If you've never heard the siren call of a warm brownie, I'm not going to try to explain it to you."

BROWNIES: The Earliest Aromatherapy.

TAKE ONE
And I'll bite your head off.
DiBartolo

"Oh, my. It smells wonderful in here, Iris.
Chocolate scented kitty litter?"

Assorted
Chocolates
ONE POUND
Fine
Chocolates
1
Pound
D. Barstow

"I really hope it's Boston cream pie this time."

"Did you ever notice that inner child and ice cream have the same initials? Well, I did."

County Fair
BAKING CONTEST

Lemon Bars
2nd Prize

Fudge Cake
GRAND PRIZE!

Carrot
Cups
3rd P

D. Barstow

"Double the chocolates, double the fun."

"And whenever you need a candy bar. I won't ask why, and I'll run to the store immediately."

“Let’s go someplace with chocolate mole on the menu. Olé.”

"Does this come in liquid form?"

"Mother, they're **still** Toll House cookies, even with a different brand of chocolate chip."

"Who goest there? And are you bearing gifts of bittersweet chocolate, and if not, why not?"

HER
HER
HER
HER
HER
One Gallon Chocolate Syrup.
Because you can never
have too much of it, if you
know what we're getting at,
and we think that you do...
D. Barstow

"I know things look bad now, Louise. But you can either curse the darkness, or pigout on chocolate."

"Okay, now who gets the herb tea, and who gets the entire triple chocolate mousse cake?"

"This was a great year for chocolate, wasn't it."

"*Doris*! Your Pudding-of-the-Month Club is here."

"Dear Betty, I regret to inform you that the pretty little cake on your *box* looked *much* better than *mine*..."

"It's your severance package. I think you'll like the missus's brownies."

MEL'S
BAKERY
D. Barstow

"Honey, I give up. Where's that last piece of chocolate cake?"

I'll have the tossed green salad. And hold the dressing.

A hot fudge sundae, please. With extra whipped cream and nuts.

D. Barstow

The divine drink which builds up resistance and fights fatigue. A cup of this precious drink permits man to walk for a whole day without food.

- Hernando Cortés, *1519*

No other factory in the world mixes its chocolate by waterfall.

- Willy Wonka and the Chocolate Factory

Forget love, I'd rather fall in chocolate.

- Anonymous

"I'm looking for a man who believes in quality chocolate. Not the drugstore kind."

"Anywhere with a view of the dessert cart is fine."

SUNDAE DRIVERS.

WHAT FAT WOMEN DAYDREAM ABOUT.

WHAT THIN WOMEN DAYDREAM ABOUT.

D. Barstow

1. CHOCOLATE 2. THE KIDS
D. Barstow

"Mom says 'devil's food cake' isn't cussing.
She says actually, it's a kind of prayer."

My good. My bad.
Beaucoup Chocolates
D. Barstow

CUPID'S EVIL TWIN BROTHER.

D. Barstow

"Well, we're almost out of time, but before I give you the recipe for World's Best Truffle Cake, let me tell you the history of chocolate. It was discovered in the 1500's by the Aztecs, a people..."

The Sweet Tooth
FRESH TRUFFLES TODAY!
D. Barstow

"Hon? I just broke open the chocolate soap...come help me suds up!"

"...but I think of it as healthy! It's made with beans, right? All right, it's cocoa beans..."

"Guess what, my cleaning lady got into my chocolate stash. How do you think I should handle it?"

"Uh, oh, what's this... some kind of global disaster... but I still see a nice chocolatey something coming your way."

"Nope, not chocolate covered, just regular."

Is that ganache?
Gesundheit.
D. Barstow

"Hey, hey, how come I always gotta be the mediator around here?"

“And would the lady or the gentleman like a kiss?”

“The candy weighed an ounce, but I gain a pound.
I’m going to write to my congressperson.”

801.29
Another chocolate smudge.
Cadbury, I believe.
Fine: 25 cents!
RETURNS

“Let’s talk about matters of the heart. Who here would rather talk about chocolate than passion?”

"How many salads do I have to eat before I can get dessert?"

"Grandma, I'm **still** waiting for your secret recipe for Cocoa Sponge Cake! Grandma. **GRANDMA?**

Let them eat cake! And don't stint on the icing and non-pareils.
D Barstow

"Little Debbie. Sara Lee. Betty Crocker. I miss them all, my sweet ladies."

Ice Cream for Dummies.

You know what they say,
the higher the hat....
the higher the cake.
D. Barstow

Chocolate is a divine, celestial drink, the sweat of the stars, the vital seed, divine nectar, the drink of the gods, panacea and universal medicine.

- ***Geronimo Piperni,*** *quoted by Antonio Lavedán, surgeon in the Spanish army, 1796*

It's not that chocolates are a substitute for love. Love is a substitute for chocolate. Chocolate is, let's face it, far more reliable than a man.

- ***Miranda Ingram***

There are four basic food groups: milk chocolate, dark chocolate, white chocolate, and chocolate truffles.

- ***Anonymous***

D. Barstow

"I cannot tell a lie. Forget the cherry pie.
Cherish the chocolate cheesecake."

"Mom, tell me again about the blue ribbons Grandma won at the State Fair for her Black Forest Cake."

"It's a vitamin C and a B complex. Didn't they use to put **mints** on the pillows?"

"I'm told it's solid chocolate."

VISTA
CHOCOLATE: THE MOVIE
FULL COLOR
NOW Showing!
D. Barstow

ANOTHER FREUDIAN SLIP.

D. Barstow

"Hey, would it **kill** them to make devil's food cake once in a while?"

“No more chocolate-flavored treats for you, mister. They’re way too tempting to have around.”

"Ha, I *thought* I smelled chocolate chip cookie dough ice cream."

"So. Mrs Hansen, if I supply you with imported chocolates, instead of apples, can we call it a deal?"

"Oh ye of little faith. You'll be happy to know that we do have chocolate down here. But it's all carob, don't you know!"

"Gary, look, a chocolate snowman! Isn't that just ironic?"

"PURGATORY."

"I think the Kama Sutra forgot hot cocoa kisss."

"Chocolate happens, dear."

"Diane, hell is paved with chocalate-covered potato chips.
Move along, people, there's nothing here to see."

"Honey? Are you awake? I have a jones for frozen custard. **Now**."

I didn't see it on the menu, but can I order a handful of M&Ms as a side dish?
D. Barstow

"Nothing makes me feel like more of a woman than buying a big block of professional baking chocalate!"

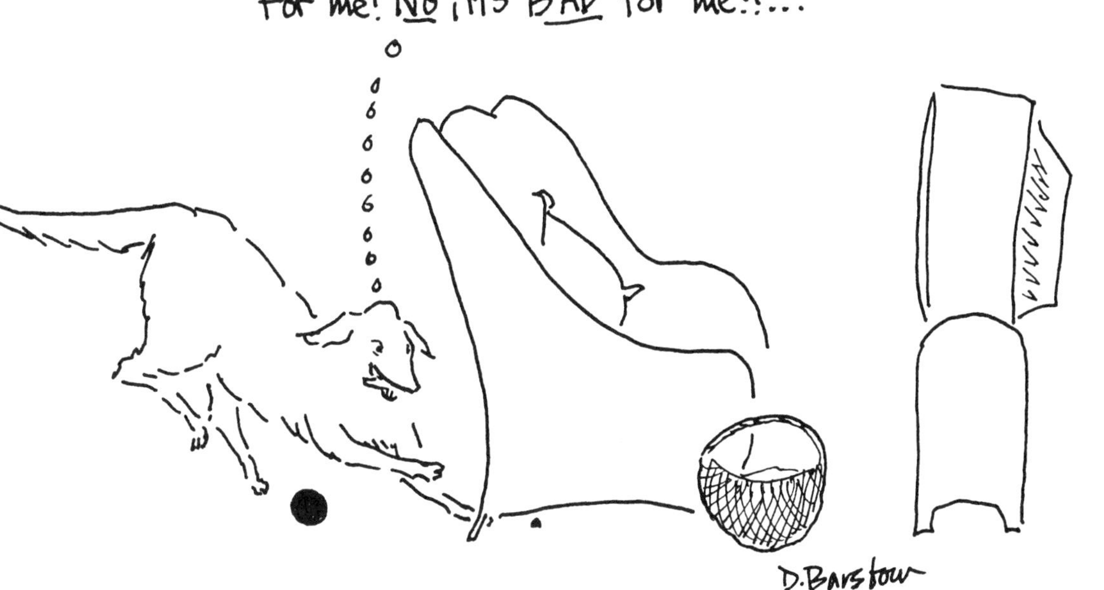
Oooh, goodie! I love chocolate!
Chocolate is GOOD for me! No, its BAD for me!! No, it's GOOD for me! No, its BAD for me!!...
D.Barstow

Choco-
Scent
P. Barstow

Hmm, this candy has raisins *and* nuts in it. Definitely part of the food pyramid...

D. Barstow

What use are cartridges in battle? I always carry chocolate instead.

- ***George Bernard Shaw,*** *1894*

The 12-step chocoholics program: NEVER BE MORE THAN 12 STEPS AWAY FROM CHOCOLATE!

- ***Terry Moore***

After about 20 years of marriage, I'm finally starting to scratch the surface of that one [what women want]. And I think the answer lies somewhere between conversation and chocolate.

- ***Mel Gibson***

She loves me!
D. Barstow

"Mom said I shouldn't register for fine chocolate, but I say first things first."

"Ice cream is an all-weather food, Roger."

"Tonight on the Discovery Channel...who found the first chocolate bon bons and how did he identify them, with all the strange swirly designs on top? Stay tuned for this one..."

"Your weight's fine. Say, have you tried Lynn's Confectioners, 1015 Central, open 10-5?"

"Honey, it's normal to crave chocolate and pickles.
But not at the same time. Get a grip."

"The only time I crave chocolate is when Neal and I have a fight. Or when we make up, to celebrate. And of course, on the major holidays, but that's a given..."

“And do you, Kevin, swear that chocolate, whether too much or too llittle, will never be an issue in this marriage?”

"There's nothing strange in the cocoa this time, I promise."

"Why not make him a tunnel of fudge cake, dear? That will bring him to his knees. And then you'll thank your lucky stars."

It beats Toto.
OZ
m
D. Barstow

"I'll take the Molten Chocolate Cake, please. And don't bring any extra fork."

“No dessert, thanks. We’re going to catch “Death by Chocolate” on tv tonight.”

"God, thank you for giving me the funds to buy fine chocolate, the wisdom to know which types to get, and the strength to put some away for later."

"I believe we have something in common. I, too, love chocolate ice cream."

"Geoff, I have like 1000 dessert recipes now. If I should die before I get to try them all, will you promise to make the rest of them?"

FATAL ATTRACTION.
(in the case of chocolate-chunk cookies)

D. Barstow

"It's that time of the month... I spent my whole lunch hour running around to chocolate shops."

"So... um... what do you think about chocolate in all its myriad forms?"

"Chocolate tastes more **gourmet** if I order it online."

"I'm making fudge for Dad's birthday. It will remind him of the boardwalk, and then he'll think of sand, and then he'll think of golf, and then he'll be happy."

"This looks good, sweetie. The first 3 ingredients listed are chocolate."

"Mom, I told you the doctor said chocolate mousse is too rich for the kids. Now we'll have to eat it ourselves again."

"For Mitch's birthday I'm giving him boxer shorts with yummy little candies all over them. Kind of a gift for both of us..."

"Todd is so hot! His hair is the color of a caramel sundae, his eyes are like dark bittersweet glaze, and he kisses like the froth on a chocolate soda! Yummy!"

It has been shown as proof positive that carefully prepared chocolate is as healthful a food as it is pleasant; that it is nourishing and easily digested... that it is above all helpful to people who must do a great deal of mental work.

- Anthelme Brillat-Savarin
(French magistrate and gastronome)

All I really need is love, but a little chocolate now and then doesn't hurt!

- Lucy Van Pelt *in Peanuts by Charles M. Schulz*

My therapist told me the way to achieve true inner peace is to finish what I start. So far today, I have finished 2 bags of M&M's and a chocolate cake. I feel better already.

- Dave Barry

Bye, hon,
just going out
to get Vitamin C.
Vitamin C
means
Chocolate.
D. Barstow

"I hope they don't make any personal comments this time about my backpack of emergency chocolate..."

"Cold ice cream, warm heart."

"Who knew? There is a pot of gold coins! And it's all chocolate... and it's all mine!"

“Kevin, if you’ve never heard the siren call of a warm brownie. I’m not going to try to explain it to you.”

"That's my collection of candy boxes. They don't hold much, but sweet memories..."

"I don't care about a guy's car, or job, or if he brings me flowers...
but he's gotta have chocolate to stay in the race!"

“And this will be a climate-controlled room for our art and chocolate collections.”

"Just a thought... if I made black and white cookies for the judge, would he think I was being anything besides kind?"

"I hate summer. Chocolate melts at body temperature, and so do I..."

"Bye, kids, and enjoy your **full-size** candybars. **Some** of us still have integrity!"

"That's what I love about chocolate... it doesn't need anything else to be perfect. It stands alone just fine."

“That’s not true, Mom. Weight Watchers never explicitly says ‘no chocolate’.”

"I know you've cut back, but they promised me you'd still have Junior Mints and popcorn for the movie."

Karma's Pizzeria

Where dreams come true... anything you want on it... even chocolate!

DBarstow

"They all look delicious. How many could I eat before I implode?"

"Why do we always end up with **vanilla**? Where is the justice here?"

"That's what we need this winter... More chocolatey Ovaltine, Mom!"

"I was seduced today by a new chocolate bar. It kept calling me, in its pretty wrapper, so I smelled it and finally broke down and took a bite, and then another... I don't regret a single thing."

"When did love become a substitute for chocolate, or is it the other way around? And can't we have both?"

Make Your Own Sundae!

Cara Syrup

Whip Crea

D.Barstow

"Hard-boiled, with a creamy chocolate center, please."